This Book Belongs to:

Thanks for your purchase!
We hope you enjoy this Journal.
If you consider this notebook
useful please leave a review.

Thank for your support.
You are Awesome!

Made in the USA
Las Vegas, NV
11 September 2021

30046789R00070